# THE PERFECT GENTLEMAN

# *The*
# PERFECT GENTLEMAN

BY

RALPH   BERGENGREN

*Essay Index Reprint Series*

BOOKS FOR LIBRARIES PRESS, INC.
FREEPORT, NEW YORK

First published 1919
Reprinted 1967

PRINTED IN THE UNITED STATES OF AMERICA

# CONTENTS

## THE PERFECT GENTLEMAN

SOMEWHERE in the back of every man's mind there dwells a strange wistful desire to be thought a Perfect Gentleman. And this is much to his credit, for the Perfect Gentleman, as thus wistfully contemplated, is a high ideal of human behavior, although, in the narrower but honest admiration of many, he is also a Perfect Ass. Thus, indeed, he comes down the centuries — a sort of Siamese Twins, each miraculously visible only to its own admirers; a worthy personage proceeding at one end of the connecting cartilage, and a popinjay prancing at the other. Emerson was, and described, one twin when he wrote, 'The gentleman is a man of truth, lord of his own actions, and expressing that lordship in his behavior;

I

not in any manner dependent or servile, either on persons, or opinions, or possessions.' Walter Pater, had Leonardo painted a Perfect Gentleman's portrait instead of a Perfect Lady's, might have described the other: 'The presence that thus rose so strangely beside the tea-table is expressive of what in the ways of a thousand years women had come to desire. His is the head upon which "all the ends of the world have come," and the eyelids are a little weary. He is older than the tea things among which he sits.' Many have admired, but few have tried to imitate, the Perfect Gentleman of Emerson's definition; yet few there are who have not felt the wistful desire for resemblance. But the other is more objective: his clothes, his manners, and his habits are easy to imitate.

Of this Perfect Gentleman in the eighteenth century I recently discovered fossil remains in the *Gentleman's Pocket Library* (Boston and Philadelphia, 1794), from which any literary savant may restore the original. All in one volume, the Library is a compilation for Perfect Gentlemen in the shell, especially helpful with its chapter on the 'Principles of Politeness'; and many an honest but foolish youth went about, I dare say, with this treasure distending his pocket, bravely hoping to become a Perfect Gentleman by sheer diligence of spare-time study. If by chance this earnest student met an acquaintance who had recently become engaged, he would remember the 'distinguishing diction that marks the man of fashion,' and would 'advance with warmth and cheerfulness, and perhaps squeezing him by the hand' (oh, horror!) 'would say, "Believe me, my dear sir, I have scarce words to express the joy I feel, upon

3

your happy alliance with such and such a family, etc."' Of which distinguishing diction, 'believe *me*' is now all that is left.

If, however, he knew that the approaching victim had been lately bereaved, he would 'advance slower, and with a peculiar composure of voice and countenance, begin his compliments of condolence with, "I hope, sir, you will do me the justice to be persuaded, that I am not insensible to your unhappiness, that I take part in your distress, and shall ever be affected when *you* are so."'

In lighter mood this still imperfect Perfect Gentleman would never allow himself to laugh, knowing, on the word of his constant pocket-companion, that laughter is the 'sure sign of a weak mind, and the manner in which low-bred men express their silly joy, at silly

things, and they call it being merry.'
Better *always*, if necessary, the peculiar
composure of polite sensibility to the
suffering of properly introduced ac-
quaintances. When he went out, he
would be careful to 'walk well, wear his
hat well, move his head properly, and
his arms gracefully'; and I for one sym-
pathize with the low-breds if they found
him a merry spectacle; when he went
in, he would remember pertinently that
'a well-bred man is known by his manner of sitting.' 'Easy in every position,'
say the Principles of Politeness, 'instead
of lolling or lounging as he sits, he leans
with elegance, and by varying his atti-
tudes, shows that he has been used to
good company.' Good company, one
judges, must have inclined to be rather
acrobatic.

Now, in the seventeen-nineties there
were doubtless purchasers for the *Gen-*

*tleman's Pocket Library:* the desire to become a Perfect Gentleman (like this one) by home study evidently existed. But, although I am probably the only person who has read that instructive book for a very long time, it remains to-day the latest complete work which any young man wishing to become a Perfect Gentleman can find to study. Is it possible, I ask myself, that none but burglars any longer entertain this ambition? I can hardly believe it. Yet the fact stands out that, in an age truly remarkable for its opportunities for self-improvement, there is nothing later than 1794 to which I can commend a crude but determined inquirer. To my profound astonishment I find that the Correspondence-School system offers no course; to my despair I search the magazines for graphic illustration of an Obvious Society Leader confiding to an Obvious Scrubwoman: 'Six months ago *my* husband was no more a Perfect Gentleman than *yours*, but one day I persuaded him to *mark that coupon*, and all our social prominence and *éclat* we owe to that school.'

One may say, indeed, that here is something which cannot conceivably be described as a job; but all the more does it seem, logically, that the correspondence schools must be daily creating candidates for what naturally would be a post-graduate course. One would imagine that a mere announcement would be sufficient, and that from all the financial and industrial centres of the country students would come flocking back to college in the next mail.

BE A PERFECT GENTLEMAN

In the Bank—at the Board of Directors — putting through that New Railroad in Alaska — wherever you are and whatever you are doing to drag down the Big Money — would n't you feel more at ease if you *knew* you were behaving like a Perfect Gentleman?

We will teach YOU how.

Some fifty odd years ago Mr. George H. Calvert (whom I am pained to find recorded in the *Dictionary of American Authors* as one who 'published a great number of volumes of verse that was never mistaken for poetry by any reader') wrote a small book about gentlemen, fortunately in prose and not meant for beginners, in which he cited Bayard, Sir Philip Sidney, Charles Lamb, Brutus, St. Paul, and Socrates as notable examples. Perfect Gentlemen all, as Emerson would agree, I question if any of them ever gave a moment's thought to his manner of sitting; yet any two, sitting together, would have recognized each other as Perfect Gentlemen at once and thought no more about it.

These are the standard, true to Emerson's definition; and yet such shining examples need not discourage the rest of us. The qualities that made them gentlemen are not necessarily the qualities that made them famous. One need not be as polished as Sidney, but one must not scratch. One need not have a mind like Socrates: a gentleman may be reasonably perfect, — and surely this is not asking too much, — with mind enough to follow this essay. Brutus gained nothing as a gentleman by assisting at the assassination of Cæsar (who was no more a gentleman, by the way, in Mr. Calvert's opinion, than was Mr. Calvert a poet in that of the *Dictionary of Authors*).

As for Fame, it is quite sufficient — and this only out of gentlemanly consideration for the convenience of others — for a Perfect Gentleman to have his name printed in the Telephone Directory. And in this higher definition I go so far as to think that the man is rare who is not sometimes a Perfect Gentleman, and equally uncommon who never is anything else. Adam I hail a Perfect Gentleman when, seeing what his wife had done, he bit back the bitter words he might have said, and then — he too — took a bite of the apple: but oh! how far he fell immediately afterward, when he stammered his pitiable explanation that the woman tempted him and he did eat! Bayard, Sir Philip Sidney, Charles Lamb, St. Paul, or Socrates would have insisted, and stuck to it, that *he bit it first*.

I have so far left out of consideration — as for that matter did the author and editor of the *Pocket Library* (not wish-

ing to discourage students) — a qual-
ification essential to the Perfect Gentleman in the eighteenth century. He
must have had — what no book could
give him — an ancestor who knew how
to sit. Men there were whose social
status was visibly signified by the abbreviation 'Gent.' appended to their
surnames. But already this was becoming a vermiform appendix, and the nineteenth century did away with it. This
handsome abbreviation created an invi-
dious distinction between citizens which
democracy refused longer to countenance; and, much as a Lenin would de-
stroy the value of money in Russia by
printing countless rouble notes without
financial backing, so democracy de-
stroyed the distinctive value of the word
'gentleman' by applying it indiscrimi-
nately to the entire male population of
the United States.

# THE PERFECT GENTLEMAN

The gentleman continues in various degrees of perfection. There is no other name for him, but one hears it rarely; yet the shining virtue of democratization is that it has produced a kind of tacit agreement with Chaucer's Parson that 'to have pride in the gentrie of the bodie is right gret folie; for ofttime the gentrie of the bodie benimeth the gentrie of the soul; and also we be all of one fader and one moder.' And although there are few men nowadays who would insist that they *are* gentlemen, there is probably no man living in the United States who would admit that he is n't.

And so I now see that my bright dream of a Correspondence-School postgraduate course cannot be realized. No bank president, no corporation director, electrical engineer, advertising expert, architect, or other distinguished alumnus would confess himself no gentleman by *marking that coupon.* The suggestion would be an insult, were it affectionately made by the good old president of his Alma Mater in a personal letter. A few decorative cards, to be hung up in the office, might perhaps be printed and mailed at graduation.

A bath *every* day
Is the Gentleman's way.

Don't break the Ten Commandments —
Moses meant YOU!

Dress Well — Behave Better.

A Perfect Gentleman has a Good Heart,
a Good Head, a Good Wardrobe,
and a Good Conscience.

## AS A MAN DRESSES

A T some time or other, I dare say, it is common experience for a man to feel indignant at the necessity of dressing himself. He wakes in the morning. Refreshed with sleep, ready and eager for his daily tasks and pleasures, he is just about to leap out of bed when the thought confronts him that he must put on his clothes. His leap is postponed indefinitely, and he gets up with customary reluctance. One after another, twelve articles — eleven, if two are joined in union one and inseparable — must be buttoned, tied, laced, and possibly safety-pinned to his person: a routine business, dull, wearisome with repetition. His face and hands must be washed, his hair and teeth brushed: many, indeed, will perform all over what Keats, thinking of the ocean eternally washing the land, has called a 'priestlike task of pure ablution'; but others, faithful to tradition and Saturday night, will dodge this as wasteful. Downstairs in summer is his hat; in winter, his hat, his overcoat, his muffler, and, if the weather compels, his galoshes and perhaps his ear-muffs or ear-bobs. Last thing of all, the Perfect Gentleman will put on his walking-stick; somewhere in this routine he will have shaved and powdered, buckled his wrist-watch, and adjusted his spats.

When we think of the shortness of life, and how, even so, we might improve our minds by study between getting up and breakfast, dressing, as educators are beginning to say of the long summer vacation, seems a sheer 'wastage of education'; yet the plain truth is that we would n't get up. Better, if we

can, to *think* while we dress, pausing to
jot down our worth-while thoughts on
a handy tablet. Once, I remember, —
and perhaps the pleasant custom continues, — a lady might modestly express her kindly feeling for a gentleman
(and her shy, half-humorous recognition of the difference between them) by
giving him shaving-paper; why not a
somewhat similar tablet, to record his
dressing-thoughts?

'Clothes,' so wrote Master Thomas
Fuller, — and likely enough the idea
occurred to him some morning while
getting into his hose and doublet, —
'ought to be our remembrancers of our
lost innocency.' And so they are; for
Adam must have bounded from bed to
breakfast with an innocency that nowadays we can only envy.

Yet, in sober earnest, the first useful
thing that ever this naked fellow set his

hand to was the making of his own apron. The world, as we know and love it, began — your pardon, Mr. Kipling, but I cannot help it — when

Cross-legged our Father Adam sat and fastened
    them one by one,
Till, leaf by leaf, with loving care he got his
    apron done;
The first new suit the world had seen, and might-
    ily pleased with it,
Till the Devil chuckled behind the Tree, 'It's
    pretty, but will it fit?'

From that historic moment everything a man does has been preceded by dressing, and almost immediately the process lost its convenient simplicity. Not since Adam's apron has any complete garment, or practical suit of clothes, been devised — except for sea-bathing — that a busy man could slip on in the morning and off again at night. All our indignation to the contrary, we prefer the complicated and difficult: we enjoy our buttons; we are withheld only by our queer sex-pride from wearing garments that button up in the back — indeed, on what we frankly call our 'best clothes,' we *have the buttons* though we *dare not button* with them. The one costume that a man could slip on at night and off again in the morning has never, if he could help it, been worn in general society, and is now outmoded by a pretty little coat and pantaloons of soft material and becoming color. We come undressed; but behold! thousands of years before we were born, it was decided that we must be dressed as soon as possible afterward, and clothes were made for us while it was yet in doubt whether we would be a little gentleman or a little lady. And so a man's first clothes are cunningly fashioned to do for either; worse still, — a crying indignity that, oh, thank Heaven, he cannot remember in maturity, — he is forcibly valeted by a woman, very likely young and attractive, to whom he has never been formally introduced.

But with this nameless, speechless, and almost invertebrate thing that he once was — this little kicking Maeterlinck (if I may so call it) between the known and the unknown worlds — the mature self-dresser will hardly concern himself. Rather, it may be, will he contemplate the amazing revolution which, in hardly more than a quarter-century, has reversed public opinion, and created a free nation which, no longer regarding a best-dresser with fine democratic contempt, now seeks, with fine democratic unanimity, to be a best-dresser itself. Or perhaps, smiling, he will recall Dr. Jaeger, that brave and lonely spirit who sought to persuade us that no other garment is so comfortable, so hygienic, so convenient, and so becoming to all figures, as the union suit — and that it should be worn externally, with certain modifications to avoid arrest. His photograph, thus attired, is stamped on memory: a sensible, bearded gentleman, inclining to stoutness, comfortably dressed in eye-glasses and a modified union suit. And then, almost at the same moment, the Clothing Industry, perhaps inspired by the doctor's courage and informed by his failure, started the revolution, since crowned by critical opinion, in a Sunday newspaper, that 'The American man, considering him in all the classes that constitute American society, is to-day the best-dressed, best-kept man in the world.'

Forty or fifty years ago no newspaper could plausibly have made that statement, and, if it had, its office would probably have been wrecked by a mob of insulted citizens; but the Clothing Industry knew us better than Dr. Jaeger, better even than we knew ourselves. Its ideal picture of a handsome, snappy young fellow, madly enjoying himself in exquisitely fitting, ready-to-wear clothes, stirred imaginations that had been cold and unresponsive to the doctor's photograph. We admired the doctor for his courage, but we admired the handsome, snappy young fellow for his looks; nay, more, we jumped in multitudes to the conclusion, which has since been partly borne out, that ready-to-wear clothes would make us all look like him. And so, in all the classes that constitute American society (which I take to include everybody who wears a collar), the art of dressing, formerly restricted to the few, became popular with the many. Other important and necessary industries — the hatters, the

shoemakers, the shirtmakers, the cra-
vatters, the hosiers, even the makers of
underwear — hurried out of hiding; and
soon, whoever had eyes to look could
study that handsome, snappy young
fellow in every stage of costume, — for
the soap-makers also saw their opportunity, — from the bath up.

The tailor survived, thanks probably
to the inevitable presence of Doubting
Thomas in any new movement; but he,
too, has at last seen the light. I read
quite recently his announcement that
in 1919 men's clothes would be 'sprightly without conspicuousness; dashing
without verging on extremes; youthful in temperament and inspirational.'
Some of us, it appears, remain self-con-
scious and a little afraid to snap; and
there the tailor catches us with his
cunningly conceived 'sprightly without
conspicuousness.' Unlike the *vers-libre*

poetess who would fain 'go naked in the
street and walk unclothed into people's
parlors,' — leaving, one imagines, an
idle but deeply interested gathering on
the sidewalk, — we are timid about extremes. We wish to dash — but within
reasonable limits. Nor, without forcing
the note, would we willingly miss an
opportunity to inspire others, or commit the affectation of concealing a still
youthful temperament.

A thought for the tablet: *As a man
dresses, so he is.*

Thirty or forty years ago there were
born, and lived in a popular magazine,
two gentlemen-heroes whose perfect
friendship was unmarred by rivalry because, like Rosencranz and Guilden-
stern, they were of such different but
equally engaging types of manly beauty. I forget whether they married sis-
ters, but they live on in the memory as

ornamental symbols of a vanished past
— a day when fiction-writers impressed
it, on their readers with every means at
their command, that a hero was well-
dressed, well-washed, and well-groomed.
Such details have become unnecessary,
and grumpy stand-patters no longer
contemptuously mutter, 'Soap! Soap!'
when a hero comes down to breakfast.
Some of our older politicians, to be sure,
still wear a standard costume of Prince
Albert coat, pants (for so one must call
them) that bag at the knee, and an im-
personal kind of black necktie, sleeping,
I dare say, in what used jocularly to
be called a 'nightie'; but our younger
leaders go appropriately clad, to the
eye, in exquisitely fitting, ready-to-wear
clothes. So, too, does the Correspondence-School graduate, rising like an
escaped balloon from his once precari-
ous place among the untrained workers

to the comfortable security of general manager. Here and there, an echo of the past, persists the pretence that men are superior to any but practical considerations in respect to clothing; but if this were so, I need hardly point out that more would dress like Dr. Jaeger, and few waste precious moments fussing over the selection of prettily colored ribbons to wear round their necks.

Fortunately we need no valets, and a democracy of best-dressers is neither more nor less democratic than one of shirt-sleeves: the important thing in both cases is that the great majority of citizens all look alike. The alarm-clock awakens us, less politely than a James or Joseph, but we need never suspect it of uncomplimentary mental reservations, and neither its appetite nor its morals cause us uneasiness. Fellow-citizens of Greek extraction maintain parlors where we may sit, like so many statues on the Parthenon, while they polish our shoes. In all large cities are quiet retreats where it is quite conventional, and even *dégagé*, for the most Perfect Gentleman to wait in what still remains to him, while an obliging fellow creature swiftly presses his trousers; or, lacking this convenient retreat, there are shrewd inventions that crease while we sleep. Hangers, simulating our own breadth of shoulders, wear our coats and preserve their shape. Wooden feet, simulating our own honest trotters, wear our shoes and keep them from wrinkling. No valet could do more. And as for laying out our clothes, has not the kind Clothing Industry provided handy manuals of instruction? With their assistance any man can lay out the garments proper to any function, be it a morning dig in the garden, a noon wedding at the White House, or (if you can conceive it) a midnight supper with Mrs. Carrie Nation.

And yet — sometimes, that indignation we feel at having to dress ourselves in the morning, we feel again at having to undress ourselves at night. Then indeed are our clothes a remembrancer of our lost innocency. We think only of Adam going to bed. We forget that, properly speaking, poor innocent Adam had no bed to go to. And we forget also that in all the joys of Eden was none more innocent than ours when we have just put on a new suit.

## IN THE CHAIR

ABOUT once in so often a man must go to the barber for what, with contemptuous brevity, is called a haircut. He must sit in a big chair, a voluminous bib (prettily decorated with polka dots) tucked in round his neck, and let another human being cut his hair for him. His head, with all its internal mystery and wealth of thought, becomes for the time being a mere poll, worth two dollars a year to the tax-assessor: an irregularly shaped object, between a summer squash and a cantaloupe, with too much hair on it, as very likely several friends have advised him. His identity vanishes.

As a rule, the less he now says or thinks about his head, the better: he has given it to the barber, and the barber

will do as he pleases with it. It is only
when the man is little and is brought in
by his mother, that the job will be done
according to instructions; and this is
because the man's mother is in a position to see the back of his head. Also
because the weakest woman under such
circumstances has strong convictions.
When the man is older the barber will
sometimes allow him to see the haircut cleverly reflected in two mirrors;
but not one man in a thousand — nay,
in ten thousand — would dare express
himself as dissatisfied. After all, what
does he know of haircuts, he who is no
barber? Women feel differently; and I
know of one man who, returning home
with a new haircut, was compelled to
turn round again and take what his
wife called his 'poor' head to another
barber by whom the haircut was more
happily finished. But that was excep-

tional. And it happened to that man but once.

The very word 'haircut' is objectionable. It snips like the scissors. Yet it describes the operation more honestly than the substitute 'trim,' a euphemism that indicates a jaunty habit of dropping in frequently at the barber's and so keeping the hair perpetually at just the length that is most becoming. For most men, although the knowledge must be gathered by keen, patient observation and never by honest confession, there is a period, lasting about a week, when the length of their hair is admirable. But it comes between haircuts. The haircut itself is never satisfactory. If his hair was too long before (and on this point he has the evidence of unprejudiced witnesses), it is too short now. It must grow steadily — count on it for that! — until for a

brief period it is 'just right,' æstheti-
cally suited to the contour of his face
and the cut of his features, and beginning already imperceptibly to grow too
long again.

Soon this growth becomes visible,
and the man begins to worry. 'I must
go to the barber,' he says in a harassed
way. 'I must get a haircut.' But the
days pass. It is always to-morrow, and
to-morrow, and to-morrow. When he
goes, he goes suddenly.

There is something within us, probably our immortal soul, that postpones
a haircut; and yet in the end our immortal souls have little to do with the
actual process. It is impossible to conceive of one immortal soul cutting another immortal soul's hair. My own
soul, I am sure, has never entered a
barber's shop. It stops and waits for
me at the portal. Probably it converses,

on subjects remote from our bodily consciousness, with the immortal souls of barbers, patiently waiting until the barbers finish their morning's work and come out to lunch.

Even during the haircut our hair is still growing, never stopping, never at rest, never in a hurry: it grows while we sleep, as was proved by Rip Van Winkle. And yet perhaps sometimes it is in a hurry; perhaps that is why it falls out. In rare cases the contagion of speed spreads; the last hair hurries after all the others; the man is emancipated from dependence on barbers. I know a barber who is in this independent condition himself (for the barber can no more cut his own hair than the rest of us) and yet sells his customers a preparation warranted to keep them from attaining it: a seeming anomaly which can be explained only on the ground that business is business. To escape the haircut one must be quite without hair that one cannot see and reach; and herein possibly is the reason for a fashion which has often perplexed students of the Norman Conquest. The Norman soldiery wore no hair on the backs of their heads; and each brave fellow could sit down in front of his polished shield and cut his own hair without much trouble. But the scheme had a weakness; the back of the head had to be shaved; and the fashion doubtless went out because, after all, nothing was gained by it. One simply turned over on one's face in the barber's chair instead of sitting up straight.

Fortunately we begin having a haircut when we are too young to think, and when also the process is sugar-coated by the knowledge that we are losing our curls. Then habit accustoms us to it. Yet it is significant that men of refinement seek the barber in secluded places, basements of hotels for choice, where they can be seen only by barbers and by other refined men having or about to have haircuts; and that men of less refinement submit to the operation where every passer-by can stare in and see them, bibs round their necks and their shorn locks lying in pathetic little heaps on the floor. There is a barber's shop of this kind in Boston where one of the barbers, having no head to play with, plays on a cornet, doubtless to the further distress of his immortal soul peeping in through the window. But this is unusual even in the city that is known far and wide as the home of the Boston Symphony Orchestra.

I remember a barber — he was the only one available in a small town —

who cut my left ear. The deed distressed him, and he told me a story. It was a pretty little cut, he said, — filling it with alum, — and reminded him of another gentleman whose left ear he had nipped in identically the same place. He had done his best with alum and apology, as he was now doing. Two months later the gentleman came in again. 'And by golly!' said the barber, with a kind of wonder at his own cleverness, 'if I did n't nip him again in just the same place!'

A man can shave himself. The Armless Wonder does it in the Dime Museum. Byron did it, and composed poetry during the operation; although, as I have recently seen scientifically explained, the facility of composition was not due to the act of shaving but to the normal activity of the human mind at that time in the morning. Here, therefore, a man can refuse the offices of the barber. If he wishes to make one of a half-dozen apparently inanimate figures, their faces covered with soap, and their noses used as convenient handles to turn first one cheek and then the other — that is his own look-out. But human ingenuity has yet to invent a 'safety barber's shears.' It has tried. A near genius once invented an apparatus — a kind of helmet with multitudinous little scissors inside it — which he hopefully believed would solve the problem; but what became of him and his invention I have not heard. Perhaps he tried it himself and slunk, defeated, into a deeper obscurity. Perhaps he committed suicide; for one can easily imagine that a man who thought he had found a way to cut his own hair and then found that he had n't, would be thrown into a suicidal depression.

36

## IN THE CHAIR

There is the possibility that he succeeded in cutting his own hair, and was immediately 'put away,' by his sensitive family where nobody could see him but the hardened attendants. The important fact is that the invention never got on the market. Until some other investigator succeeds to more practical purpose, the rest of us must go periodically to the barber. We must put on the bib —

Here, however, there is at least an opportunity of selection. There are bibs with arms, and bibs without arms. And there is a certain amount of satisfaction in being able to see our own hands, carefully holding the newspaper or periodical wherewith we pretend that we are still intelligent human beings. And here again are distinctions. The patrons of my own favored barber's shop have arms to their bibs and pretend to be deeply interested in the *Illustrated London News*. The patrons of the barber's shop where I lost part of my ear — I cannot see the place, but those whom I take into my confidence tell me that it has long since grown again — had no sleeves to their bibs, but nevertheless managed awkwardly to hold the *Police Gazette*. And this opportunity to hold the *Police Gazette* without attracting attention becomes a pleasant feature of this type of barber's shop: I, for example, found it easier — until my ear was cut — to forget my position in the examination of this journal than in the examination of the *Illustrated London News*. The pictures, strictly speaking, are not so good, either artistically or morally, but there is a tang about them, an I-do-not-know-what. And it is always wisest to focus attention on some such extraneous interest. Otherwise you may get to looking in the mirror.

Do not do that.

For one thing, there is the impulse to cry out, 'Stop! Stop! Don't cut it all off!

> 'Oh, barber, spare that hair!
> Leave some upon my brow!
> For months it's sheltered me!
> And I'll protect it now!

'Oh, please! P-l-e-a-s-e! —'

These exclamations annoy a barber, rouse a demon of fury in him. He reaches for a machine called 'clippers.' Tell him how to cut hair, will you! A little more and he'll shave your head — and not only half-way either, like the Norman soldiery at the time of the Conquest! Even if you are able to restrain this impulse, clenching your bib in your hands and perhaps dropping or tearing the *Illustrated London News*, the mirror gives you strange, morbid reflections. You recognize your face, but your head seems somehow separate, balanced on a kind of polka-dotted mountain with two hands holding the *Illustrated London News*. You are afraid momentarily that the barber will lift it off and go away with it.

Then is the time to read furiously the weekly contribution of G. K. Chesterton. But your mind reverts to a story you have been reading about how the Tulululu islanders, a savage but ingenious people, preserve the heads of their enemies so that the faces are much smaller but otherwise quite recognizable. You find yourself looking keenly at the barber to discover any possible trace of Tulululu ancestry.

And what is he going to get now? A *kris?* No, a paint-brush. Is he going to paint you? And if so — what color?

## IN THE CHAIR

The question of color becomes strangely important, as if it made any real difference. Green? Red? Purple? Blue? No, he uses the brush dry, tickling your forehead, tickling your ears, tickling your nose, tickling you under the chin and down the back of your neck. After the serious business of the haircut, a barber must have some relaxation.

There is one point on which you are independent: you will not have the bay rum; you are a teetotaller. You say so in a weak voice which nevertheless has some adamantine quality that impresses him. He humors you; or perhaps your preference appeals to his sense of business economy.

He takes off your bib.

From a row of chairs a man leaps to his feet, anxious to give *his* head to the barber. A boy hastily sweeps up the hair that was yours — already as remote from you as if it had belonged to the man who is always waiting, and whose name is Next. Oh, it is horrible — horrible — horrible!

## OH, SHINING SHOES!

IN a democracy it is fitting that a man should sit on a throne to have his shoes polished, or, to use a brighter, gayer word, shined. We are all kings, and this happy conceit of popular government is nicely symbolized by being, for these shining moments, so many kings together, each on his similar throne and with a slave at his feet. The democratic idea suffers a little from the difficulty of realizing that the slave is also a king, yet gains a little from the fair custom of the livelier monarchs of turning from left foot to right and from right to left, so that, within human limits, neither shoe shall be undemocratically shined first.

Nor is it uncommon for the kings on the thrones to be symbolically and inexpensively served by yet other sovereign servants. Newspapers in hand, they receive the reports of their lord high chancellors, digest the social gossip of their realm, review its crimes, politics, discoveries, and inventions, and are entertained by their jesters, who, I have it on the authority of a current advertisement, all democratically smoke the same kind of tobacco. 'You know 'em all, the great fun-makers of the daily press, agile-brained and nimble-witted, creators of world-famed characters who put laughter into life. Such live, virile humans as they *must* have a live, virile pipe-smoke.' There are, to be sure, some who find in this agile-brained and nimble-witted mirth an element of profound melancholy; it seems often a debased coin of humor, which rings false on the counter of intelligence; yet even at its worst it is far better than many of the

44

waggeries that once stirred laughter in mediæval monarchs. The thought renders them bearable, these live, virile humans, who only a few centuries ago would have been too handicapped by their refinement to compete successfully with contemporary humorists.

But there are a good many of us, possessors of patience, self-control, and a sponge in a bottle, who rarely enjoy this royal prerogative. We shine our own shoes. Alone, and, if one may argue from the particular to the general, simply dressed in the intermediate costume, more or less becoming, that is between getting up and going out, we wear a shoe on our left hand, and with the other manipulate the helpful sponge. Sometimes, too anxious, it polka-dots our white garments, sometimes the floor; it is safe only in the bottle, and the wisest shiner will perhaps approach the job as an Adamite, bestriding, like a colossus, a wide-spread newspaper, and taking a bath afterward. Or it may be that instead of the bottle we have a little tin box, wedded to its cover, — how often have we not exclaimed between clenched teeth, 'What man hath joined together man can pull asunder!' — and containing a kind of black mud, which we apply with an unfortunate rag or with a brush appropriately called the 'dauber.' Having daubed, we polish, breathing our precious breath on the luminous surface for even greater luminosity. The time is passing when we performed this task of pure lustration, as Keats might have called it, in the cellar or the back hall, more fully, but not completely, dressed, coatless, our waistcoats rakishly unbuttoned or vulgarly upstairs, our innocent trousers hanging on their gallowses, our shoes on our feet, and our physical

activity not altogether unlike that de-
manded by a home-exerciser to reduce
the abdomen. Men of girth have been
advised to saw wood; I wonder that they
never have been advised to shine their
own shoes — twenty-five times in the
morning and twenty-five times just before going to bed.

My own observation, although not
continuous enough to have scientific
value, leads me to think that stout men
are the more inveterate patrons of the
shoe-blacking parlor, — Cæsar should
have run one, — and that the present
popularity of the sponge in a bottle may
derive from superfluous girth. Invented
as a dainty toilet accessory for women,
and at first regarded by men as effemin-
ate, it is easy to see how insidiously the
sponge in a bottle would have attracted
a stout husband accustomed to shine
his own shoes in the earlier contortion-

ist manner. By degrees, first one stout husband and then another, men took to the bottle; the curse of effeminacy was lifted; the habit grew on men of all sizes. It was not a perfect method, — it blacked too many other things besides shoes, and provided an undesirable plaything for baby, — but it was a step forward. There was a refinement, a *je ne sais quoi*, an 'easier way,' about this sponge in a bottle; and, perhaps more than all, a delusive promise that the stuff would dry shiny without friction, which appealed to the imagination.

Then began to disappear a household familiar — that upholstered, deceptive, utilitarian hassock kind of thing which, when opened, revealed an iron foot-rest, a box of blacking, — I will not *say* how some moistened that blacking, but you and I, gentle reader, brought water in a crystal glass from the kitchen, —

and an ingenious tool which combined the offices of dauber and shiner, so that one never knew how to put it away right side up. This tool still exists, an honest, good-sized brush carrying a round baby brush pickaback; and I dare say an occasional old-fashioned gentleman shines his shoes with it; but in the broader sense of that pernicious and descriptive phrase it is no longer used 'by the best people.' Of late, I am told by shopkeepers, the tin box with the pervicacious cover is becoming popular; but I remain true to my sponge in a bottle; for, unlike the leopard, I am able to change my spots.

Looking along the ages from the vantage of a throne in the shoe-blacking parlor, it is a matter of pleased wonder to observe what the mind has found to do with the feet; nor is the late invention of shoe-polish (hardly earlier than the

Declaration of Independence) the least surprising item. For the greater part of his journey man has gone about his businesses in unshined footwear, beginning, it would appear, with a pair of foot-bags, or foot-purses, each containing a valuable foot, and tied round the ankle. Thus we see him, far down the vista of time, a tiny figure stopping on his way to tie up his shoe-strings. Captivated with form and color, he exhausted his invention in shapes and materials before ever he thought of polish: he cut his toes square; he cut his toes so long and pointed that he must needs tie them to his knee to keep from falling over them; he wore soles without uppers, — alas! poor devil, how often in all ages has he approximated wearing uppers without soles! — and he went in for top-boots splendidly belegged and coquettishly beautified with what, had he been a lady, he might have described as an insertion of lace. At last came the boot-blacking parlor, late nineteenth century, commercial, practical, convenient, and an important factor in civic æsthetics. Not that the parlor is beautiful in itself. It is a cave without architectural pretensions, but it accomplishes unwittingly an important mission: it removes from public view the man who is having his shoes shined.

You know him, as the advertisement says of the live, virile humans who *must* have the live, virile pipe-smoke; but happily you know him nowadays chiefly by effort of memory. Yet only a little while ago kindly, well-intentioned men thought nothing of having their shoes shined in the full glare of the sun. The man having his shoes shined was a common spectacle. He sat or stood where anybody might see him, almost as immobile as a cigar-store Indian and much less decorative, with a peripatetic shoeblack busy at his feet. His standing attitude was a little like Washington crossing the Delaware; and when he sat down, he was not wholly unlike the picture of Jupiter in Mr. Bulfinch's well-known *Age of Fable*. He had his shoes shined on the sidewalk, congesting traffic; he had them shined in the park, with the birds singing; wherever he had them shined, he was as lacking in self-consciousness as a baby sucking its thumb. Peripatetic shoeblacks pursued pedestrians, and no sensitive gentleman was safe from them merely because he had carefully and well shined his own shoes before he came out. But how rarely nowadays do we see this peripatetic shoeblack! Soon he will be as extinct as the buffalo, and the shoe-blacking parlor is his Buffalo Bill.

## OH, SHINING SHOES!

In the shoe-blacking parlor we are all tarred with the same brush, all daubed with the same dauber; we have nothing, as the rather enigmatical phrase goes, *on* one another. Indeed, we hardly look at one another, and are as remote as strangers sitting side by side in a theatre. Individually, in a steady, subconscious way, I think we are all wondering how we are going to get down when the time comes. One will hop, like a great sparrow; another will turn round and descend backward; another will come down with an absent-minded little wave of the foot, as if he were quite used to having his shoes shined and already thinking of more serious business; another — but this is sheer nervousness and lack of *savoir-faire* — will step off desperately, as if into an abyss, and come down with a thump. Sometimes, but rarely, a man will fall off. It is a throne — and perhaps this is true of all thrones — from which no altogether self-satisfactory descent is possible; and we all know it, sitting behind our newspapers, or staring down on decadent Greece shining at our feet, or examining with curious, furtive glances those calendars the feminine beauty of which seems peculiar to shoe-blacking parlors, and has sometimes led us to wonder whether the late Mr. Comstock ever had his shoes shined.

And now, behold! the slave-king at my feet has found a long, narrow strip of linen, not, I fear, antiseptic, but otherwise suggestive of a preparedness course in first aid to the injured. He breathes on my shoes (O unhygienic shoeblack!), dulling them to make them brighter with his strip of linen. It is my notice to abdicate; he turns down the bottoms of my trousers. I do not know how I get down from the throne.

## ON MAKING CALLS

I KNOW a boy who dislikes to make calls. Making a call, he says, is 'just sitting on a chair.'

I have had the same feeling, although I had never defined it so nicely. One 'just sits on a chair' — precariously, yet with an odd sense of unhappy security, of having grown to and become part of that chair, as if one dreaded to fall off, yet strongly suspected that any real effort to get up and go away would bring the chair up and away with him. He is, so to speak, like a barnacle on a rock in an ocean of conversation. He may exhibit unbarnacle-like activity, cross and uncross his legs, fold and unfold his arms, twiddle his useful fingers, incline his tired head this way and that to relieve the strain on his neck, assume (like an actor) expressions of interest, amusement, surprise, pleasure, or what not. He may even speak or laugh. But he remains sitting on his chair. He is more and more certain that he cannot get up.

He is unlike the bottoms of his own trousers. Calmly, quietly, and by imperceptible degrees *they* get up. Higher and higher they ascend kneeward; they have an ambition to achieve the waist. Every little while he must unostentatiously, and with an easy, careless, indifferent, well-bred, and even *blasé* gesture, manage to pull them down.

I am referring, you understand, to the mature, married gentleman. Between boyhood and maturity there is a period (without which there would be fewer marriages, and perhaps none at all) when a call is a personal adventure, and it often happens that the recipient of the call, rather than the caller himself, fears that somehow or other he and his chair have grown together. But my boy friend, as I think you will agree when you consider his situation, does not, strictly speaking, call: he is taken to call. And just so is it with the average mature, married gentleman; the chief difference — and even this does not invariably hold good — is that he dresses himself. He has become part and parcel (particularly parcel) of a wise and necessary division of life in which the social end is taken over by a feminine partner. She is the expert. She knows when and where to call, what to say, and when to go home. Married, a gentleman has no further responsibilities in this business — except to come cheerfully and sit on his chair without wriggling. Sometimes, indeed, he takes a pleasure in it, but that is only when he has momentarily forgotten that he is making a call. These are his rewarding moments; and then, the first thing he knows, somebody is 'making signs' that it is time to go home!

The wise man, noticing these 'signs,' comes home. He stands not upon the order of his coming, but comes at once.

A call, says Herbert Spencer, in his *Principles of Sociology*, is 'evidently a remote sequence of that system under which a subordinate ruler had from time to time to show loyalty to a chief ruler by presenting himself to do homage.' The idea is plausible: was it not for this very reason that Cleopatra galleyed down the Cydnus to call on Antony, — a call that would probably have had a different effect on history if the lady had brought a husband, — and Sheba cameled across the desert to call on Solomon? The creditor character of the visitation survives in the common expression 'paying a call.' In both these cases, however, the calls took on a lighter and brighter aspect, a more reciprocally admiring and well-affected intimacy, than was strictly necessary to an act of political homage. One is, after all, human; and the absence of marital partners, whose presence is always a little subduing, must be taken into consideration. 'But Solomon,' you say, 'Solomon?' Sir and madam, I rise to your question. In such a situation a man with seven hundred wives is as good as a bachelor; and I think the fact that Solomon had seven hundred wives proves it.

Later the Feudal System provided natural scope for innumerable calls of this nature; visits, as we should now term them, because it was customary for the callers to bring their nighties — or would have been if the callers had had any. The Dark Ages, curiously enough, lacked this garment of the dark. But it was only after the Feudal Period that the call, as we now know and practise it, became a social custom; and even to this day feudalism, in an attenuated form, rules society, and the call is often enough an act of homage to the superior social chief. One might argue (except for the fact that Sheba *gave* as well as exhibited her treasurer to Solomon) that Mrs. Jones is but following historic precedent when she brings and exhibits Mr. Jones to Mrs. Smith. Or, again, it might be pointed out that both Cleopatra and Sheba *brought their slaves*. There is, apparently, more than one sequence (as Mr. Spencer would say), but there is also a wide divergence from original type. Only partly and occasionally an act of homage, the call has become, broadly speaking, a recognition of exact social equality, as if the round, dignified American cheese in Grocer Brown's ice-box should receive and return a call from the round, dignified American cheese in Grocer Green's ice-box.

And it has become divisible into as many varieties as Mr. Heinz's pickles. — The *call friendly* ('Let us go and call on the Smiths: I'd like to see them'); the *call compulsory* ('We really *must* make that call on the Smiths'); the *call curious* ('I wonder if it's so, what I heard yesterday about the Smiths'); the *call convenient* ('As we haven't anything better to do this evening, we might call on the Smiths); the *call proud* ('Suppose we get out the new motor, and run round to the Smiths'); and so forth, and so forth. But, however we look at it, the call is dependent upon feminine initiative. Our mature married gentleman, unless he has had already a call to the ministry, has no call, socially speaking, to make calls. It is his wife's business. As British soldiers have grimly sung on their way to battle, 'He's there because he's there, because he's there, because he's there.' But it is his plain duty to *sit on his chair*. I do not hold it legitimate in him to 'sneak off' with Mr. Smith — and smoke.

Fortunately, however, once he is there, little else is expected of him — and nothing that a man should not be willing to do for his wife. A smile, an attentive manner, the general effect of having combed his hair and washed behind his ears, a word now and then to show that he is awake (I am assuming that he controls the tendency to wriggle) — and no more is needed.

## ON MAKING CALLS

He is a lay figure, but not necessarily a lay figure of speech.

Unless a man who is taken to call is of an abnormally lively conversational habit, quick to think of something that may pass for a contribution to current thought, and even quicker to get it out, he had best accept his position as merely decorative, and try to be as decorative as possible. He should be so quick that the first words of his sentence have leaped into life before he is himself aware of what is to come hurrying after them; he may be so slow that the only sentence he has is still painfully climbing to the surface long after the proper time for its appearance has passed and been forgotten. Swallow it, my dear sir, swallow it. Silence, accompanied by a wise, appreciative glance of the eye, is better; for a man who has mastered the art of the wise look does his wife credit, and is taken home from a call with his faculties unimpaired and his self-respect undiminished: he is the same man as when he was taken out. But not so the man who starts, hesitates, and stops, as if he actually said, 'Hold-on-there-I-'ve-got-a-fine-idea — but — er — on second thought — er — I — er — that is — I guess — er — it is n't — worth hearing.'

Such a man, I say, adds little to the pleasure of himself or the company; he attracts attention only to disappoint it: and others are kind as well as sensible to ignore him. He should have kept on rapidly and developed his fine idea to the bitter end. Nor is it wise to attempt to shine, to dazzle, to surprise with a clever epigram, thoughtfully composed and tested by imaginary utterance before an imaginary charmed circle while dressing; for nothing so

64

diminishes confidence in an epigram as successive failures to get it into circulation. In calling, one must jump on the train of thought as it speeds by a way station; and there is no happy mean between jumping on a passing train and standing still on the platform — except, as I have suggested, a pleasant wave of the hand as the train passes.

'There are not many situations,' said Dr. Johnson, 'more incessantly uneasy than that in which the man is placed who is watching an opportunity to speak, without courage to take it when offered, and who, though he resolves to give a specimen of his abilities, always finds some reason or other for delaying to the next minute.'

I know that resolve; and yet how often have I, too, failed at the crucial moment to give the hoped-for specimen of my abilities! 'Not yet,' I have said to myself, 'not yet. The time is not ripe.' And so I have waited, incessantly uneasy, — as Dr. Johnson well puts it, — but always finding some reason or other to postpone the fireworks. I was beset by a kind of gross selfishness—an unwillingness to give *anybody* a specimen of my abilities. Let them chatter! Little do they guess — and never will they know — the abilities sitting on this chair! Give *them* a specimen! Yet I must confess also that my specimen seemed somehow isolated and apart from my environment. It was all right in itself, but it needed a setting; it was like a button without a coat, like an eye without a face, like a kiss without a companion.

## THE LIER IN BED

IF I had to get on with but one article of furniture, I think I would choose a bed. One could if necessary sit, eat, read, and write in the bed. In past time it has been a social centre: the hostess received in it, the guests sat on benches, and the most distinguished visitor sat on the foot of the bed. It combines the uses of all the other articles in the '$198 de luxe special 4-room outfit' that I have seen advertised for the benefit of any newly married couple with twenty dollars of their own for the first payment. Very few houses, if any, nowadays are without furniture that nobody uses, chairs that nobody ever sits on, books that nobody ever reads, ornaments that nobody ever wants, pictures that nobody ever looks at; an accumulation of unessential objects that

does credit chiefly to the activity of
manufacturers and merchants catering
to our modern lust for unnecessary ex-
penditure. Not so many centuries ago
one or two books made quite a respec-
table library; dining-room tables were
real banqueting boards laid on trestles
and taken away after the banquet; one
bench might well serve several Perfect
Gentlemen to sit upon; and a chair of
his own was the baron's privilege. To-
day the $198 de luxe special 4-room
outfit would feel naked and ashamed
without its '1 Pedestal' and '1 Piece of
Statuary.' Yet what on earth does a
happy couple, bravely starting life with
twenty dollars, want of a pedestal and a
piece of statuary? And I notice also
that the outfit — 'a complete home,'
says the description — makes no provi-
sion for a kitchen; but perhaps they are
no longer de luxe.

## THE LIER IN BED

It is impossible, at this time, to re-
cover with complete certainty the an-
tiquity of the bed. We may presume
that the Neanderthal man had a wife
(as wives were then understood) and
maintained a kind of housekeeping that
may have gone no further than pawing
some leaves together to sleep on; but
this probably was a late development.
Earlier we may imagine the wind blowing the autumn leaves together and a
Neanderthal man lying down by chance
on the pile. He found it pleasant, and,
for a few thousand years, went out of
his way to find piles of leaves to lie
down on, until one day he hit upon the
bright idea of piling the leaves together
himself. Then for the first time a man
had a bed. His sleep was localized; his
pile of leaves, brought together by his
own sedulous hands, became property.
Monogamy was encouraged, and the

69

idea of home came into being. Personally I have no doubt whatever that the man who made the first bed was so charmed with it that the practice of lying in bed in the morning began immediately; and it is probably a conservative statement that the later Pliocene era saw the custom well developed.

One wonders what the Neanderthal man would have thought of a de luxe 4-room outfit, or complete home, for $198.

Even to-day, however, there are many fortunate persons who are never awakened by an alarm-clock — that watchman's rattle, as it were, of Policeman Day. The invention is comparatively recent. Without trying to uncover the identity of the inventor, and thus adding one more to the Who's Who of Pernicious Persons, we may assume that it belongs naturally to the age of small and cheap clocks which dawned only in the nineteenth century. Some desire for it existed earlier. The learned Mrs. Carter, said Dr. Johnson, 'at a time when she was eager in study, did not awake as early as she wished, and she therefore had a contrivance that, at a certain hour, her chamber light should burn a string to which a heavy weight was suspended, which then fell with a sudden strong noise; this roused her from her sleep, and then she had no difficulty in getting up.'

This device, we judge, was peculiar to Mrs. Carter, than whom a less eager student would have congratulated herself that the sudden strong noise was over, and gone sweetly to sleep again. The venerable Bishop Ken, who believed that a man 'should take no more sleep than he can take at once,' had no need of it. He got up, we are told, at one or two o'clock in the morning 'and sometimes earlier,' and played the lute before putting on his clothes.

To me the interesting thing about these historic figures is that they got up with such elastic promptness, the one to study and the other to play the lute. The Bishop seems a shade the more eager; but there are details that Mrs. Carter would naturally have refrained from mentioning to Dr. Johnson, even at the brimming moment when he had just accepted her contribution to the *Rambler*. For most of us — or alarm-clocks would not be made to ring continuously until the harassed bed-warmer gets up and stops the racket — this getting out of bed is no such easy matter; and perhaps it will be the same when Gabriel's trumpet is the alarm-clock. We are more like Boswell, honest sleeper, and have 'thought of a pulley to raise me gradually '; and then have thought again and realized that even a pulley 'would give me pain, as it would counteract my internal disposition.' Let the world go hang; our internal disposition is to stay in bed: we cling tenaciously to non-existence — or rather, to that third state of consciousness when we are in the world but not of it.

There are those, no doubt, who will say that they have something better to do than waste their time wondering why they like to stay in bed, which they don't. They are persons who have never been bored by the monotony of dressing or have tried to vary it, sometimes beginning at one end, sometimes at the other, but always defeated by the hard fact that a man cannot button his collar until he has put on his shirt. If they condescend so far,

73

they will say, with some truth, that it is a question of weather, and any fool knows that it is not pleasant to get out of a warm bed into a cold bedroom. The matter has been considered from that angle. 'I have been warm all night,' wrote Leigh Hunt, 'and find myself in a state perfectly suited to a warm-blooded animal. To get out of this state into the cold, besides the inharmonious and uncritical abruptness of the transition, is so unnatural to such a creature that the poets, refining upon the tortures of the damned, make one of their greatest agonies consist in being suddenly transported from heat to cold — from fire to ice. They are "haled" out of their "beds," says Milton, by "harpy-footed furies" — fellows who come to call them.'

But no man, say I, or woman either, ever lay in bed and devised logical

reasons for staying there — unless for
the purposes of an essay, in which case
the recumbent essayist, snuggle as he
may, is mentally up and dressed.  He is
really awake.  He has tied his necktie.
He is a busy bee — and I can no more
imagine a busy bee lying in bed than I
can imagine lying in bed with one.  He
is no longer in the nice balance between
sense and oblivion that is too serenely
and irresponsibly comfortable to be con-
sciously analyzed; and in which, so long
as he can stay there without getting
wider awake, nothing else matters.

Lying in bed being a half-way house
between sleeping and waking, and the
mind then equally indifferent to logic
and exact realism, the lier in bed can
and does create his own dreams: it is
an inexpensive and gentlemanly pleasure.  If his bent is that way, he becomes
Big Man Me: Fortunatus's purse jingles

in his pocket; the slave jumps when he rubs the lamp; he excels in all manly sports. If you ask with what authority I can thus postulate the home-made dreams of any lier in bed but myself, the answer is easy. It is common knowledge that the half-awake minds of men thus employ themselves, and the fashion of their employment may be reasonably deduced from observation of individuals. The *ego* even of a modest man will be somewhat rampant; the *ego* of a conceited one would, barring its capability for infinite expansion, swell up and bust. But this riot of egoism has as little relation to the Fine Art of Lying in Bed as a movie play has to the fine art of the drama. The true artist may take fair advantage of his nice state of unreason to defy time and space, but he will respect essential verities. He will treat his *ego* like the child it is; and, taking example from a careful mother, tie a rope to it when he lets it out to play. Thus he will capture a kind of immortality; and his lying in bed, a transitory state itself, will contradict the transitory character of life outside of it. Companions he has known and loved will come from whatever remote places to share these moments, for the Fine Art of Lying in Bed consists largely in cultivating that inward eye with which Wordsworth saw the daffodils.

Whether this can be done on the wooden pillow of the Japanese I have no way of knowing; but I suspect there were some admirable liers in bed among the Roman patricians who were grossly accused of effeminacy because they slept on feathers.

The north of China, where bedding is laid in winter on raised platforms gently heated by little furnaces underneath, must have produced some highly cultivated liers in bed. The proverbial shortness of the German bed (which perhaps explains the German *Kultur*) may have tended to discourage the art and at the same time unconsciously stimulated a hatred of England, where the beds are proverbially generous. One can at least hope, however, that all beds are alike in this matter, provided the occupant is a proper lier, who can say fairly, —

> My bed has legs
>     To run away
> From Here and Now
>     And Everyday.
> It trots me off
>     From slumber deep
> To the Dear Land
>     Of Half-Asleep.

## TO BORE OR NOT TO BORE

TAKE me away,' said Thomas Carlyle, when silence settled for a moment over a dinner-table where one of the diners had been monologuing to the extreme limit of boredom, 'for God's sake take me away and put me in a room by myself and give me a pipe of tobacco!'

Little as we may otherwise resemble Carlyle, many of us have felt this emotion; and some realize (although the painful suspicion comes from a mind too analytical for its own comfort) that we may have occasioned it. The nice consideration for the happiness of others which marks a gentleman may even make him particularly susceptible to this haunting apprehension. Carlyle defined the feeling when he said, 'To sit still and be pumped into is never an exhilarating process.' But pumping is different. How often have I myself, my adieus seemingly done, my hat in my hand and my feet on the threshold, taken a fresh grip, hat or no hat, on the pump-handle, and set good-natured, Christian folk distressedly wondering if I would never stop! And how often have I afterward recalled something strained and morbidly intent in their expressions, a glassiness of the staring eye and a starchiness in the smiling lip, that has made me suffer under my bed-cover and swear that next time I would depart like a sky-rocket!

Truly it seems surprising, in a fortunate century when the correspondence school offers so many inexpensive educational advantages for deficient adults, that one never sees an advertisement —

# TO BORE OR NOT TO BORE

## STOP BEING A BORE!

If you *bore people* you can't be loved. *Don't you want to be loved?* Don't YOU? Then sign and mail this coupon *at once*. Let Dynamo Doit teach you through his famous mail course, *How not to be a Bore*.

The explanation, I fancy, must be that people who sign and mail coupons *at once* do not know when they are bored; that the word 'boredom,' so hopelessly heavy with sad significance to many of us, is nevertheless but caviar to the general and no bait at all for an enterprising correspondence school.

A swift survey of literature, from the Old Testament down, yields some striking discoveries. To take an example, Job does not appear to have regarded Eliphaz, Bildad, and Zophar as bores. And there is Bartlett's *Familiar Quotations*, out of which one can familiarly quote nothing about boredom earlier than Lord Byron. The subject has apparently never been studied, and the broad division into Bores Positive and Bores Negative is so recent that I have but this minute made it myself.

The Bore Positive pumps; the Bore Negative compels pumping. Unlike Carlyle, he regards being pumped into as an exhilarating process, and so, like the Old Man of the Sea on Sinbad's tired shoulders, he sits tight and says nothing; the difference being that, whereas the Old Man kept Sinbad walking, the Bore Negative keeps his victim talking. Charlie Wax—who lives down town in the shop-window and is always so well-dressed—would be a fine Bore Negative if one were left alone with him under compulsion to keep up a conversation.

Boredom, in fact, is an acquired distaste — a by-product of the printing-press and steam-engine, which between them have made and kept mankind busier than Solomon in all his wisdom could have imagined. Our arboreal ancestor could neither bore nor be bored. We see him — with the mind's eye — up there in his tree, poor stupid, his think-tank (if the reader will forgive me a word which he or she may not have *quite* accepted) practically empty; nothing but a few primal, inarticulate thinks at the bottom. It will be a million years or so yet before his progeny will say a long farewell to the old home in the tree; and even then they will lack words with which to do the occasion justice.

Language, in short, must be invented before anybody can be bored with it. And I do not believe, although I find it stated in a ten-volume Science-History of the Universe, that 'language is an internal necessity, begotten of a lustful longing to express, through the plastic vocal energy, man's secret sense of his ability to interpret Nature.' An internal necessity, yes — except in the case of the Bore Negative, who prefers to listen; but quite as likely begotten of man's anything but secret sense of his ability to interpret himself.

Speech grew slowly; and mankind, now a speaking animal, had centuries — nay, epochs — in which to become habituated to the longwindedness that Job accepted as a matter of course in Eliphaz, Bildad, and Zophar. So that even to-day many, like Job, Eliphaz, Bildad, and Zophar, bore and are bored without really knowing it.

In the last analysis a bore bores because he keeps us from something more interesting than himself. He becomes a menace to happiness in proportion as the span of life is shortened by an increasing number of things to do and places to go between crib and coffin. Coleridge's Ancient Mariner, full of an unusual personal experience that the leisurely reader finds most horridly entertaining, bored the Wedding Guest because at that moment the Wedding Guest wanted to get to the wedding, and was probably restrained from violence only by the subconscious thought that it is not good form to appear at such functions with a missing button. But the Mariner was too engrossed in his own tale to notice this lack of interest; and so invariably is the Bore Positive: everything escapes him except his listener.

But no matter how well we know when we are bored, none of us can be certain that he does not sometimes bore — not even Tammas. The one certainty is that *I may bore*, and that on the very occasion when I have felt myself as entertaining as a three-ring circus, I may in effect have been as gay and chatty as a like number of tombstones. There are persons, for that matter, who are bored by circuses and delighted by tombstones. My mistake may have been to put all my conversational eggs in one basket — which, indeed, is a very good way to bore people.

Dynamo Doit,. teaching his class of industrious correspondents, would probably write them, with a picture of himself shaking his fist to emphasize his point: 'Do not try to exhaust your subject. You will only exhaust your audience. Never talk for more than three minutes on any topic. Wear a wristwatch *and keep your eye on it*. If at the end of *three minutes* you cannot change the subject, tell one of the following anecdotes.' And I am quite sure also that Professor Doit would write to his class: 'Whatever topic you discuss, *discuss it originally*. Be apt. Be bright. Be pertinent. Be *yourself*. Remember always that it is not so much what you say as the *way you say it* that will charm your listener. Think clearly. Illustrate and drive home your meaning with illuminating figures — the sort of thing that your hearer will remember and pass on to others as "another of So-and-so's *bon-mots*." Here you will find that reading the "Wit and Humor" column in newspapers and magazines is a great help. And speak plainly. Remember that unless you are *heard* you cannot expect to *interest*. On this point, dear student, I can do no better than repeat Lord Chesterfield's advice to his son: "Read what Cicero and Quintilian say of enunciation." '

But perhaps, after all, enunciation is

no more important than renunciation; and the first virtue that we who do not wish to be bores must practise is abstemiousness of self. I know it is hard, but I do not mean total abstinence. A man who tried to converse without his *I's* would make but a blind stagger at it. This short and handsome word (as Colonel Roosevelt might have said) is not to be utterly discarded without danger of such a silence as would transform the experimenter into a Bore Negative of the most negative description. Practically deprived of speech, he would become like a Charlie Wax endowed with locomotion and provided with letters of introduction. But one can at least curb the pronoun, and, with shrewd covert glances at his wristwatch, confine the personally conducted tour into and about Myself within reasonable limits. Let him say bravely in the beginning, 'I will not talk about Myself for more than thirty minutes by my wrist-watch'; then reduce it to twenty-five; then to twenty — and so on to the irreducible minimum; and he will be surprised to feel how his popularity increases with leaps and bounds at each reduction — provided, of course, that he finds anything else to talk about.

Your Complete Bore, however, is incapable of this treatment, for he does not know that he is a bore. It is only the Occasional Bore, a sensitive, well-meaning fellow who would not harm anybody, whose head lies sleepless on a pillow hot with his blushes while he goes over and over so apt and tripping a dialogue that it would withhold Gabriel from blowing his trumpet. So it seems to him in his bed; but alas, these dialogues are never of any practical use. They comfort, but they do not cure.

For no person ever talks to us as we talk to ourselves. The better way is to decide firmly (1) to get a wrist-watch, and (2) to get to sleep.

There is, however, one infallible rule for not being a bore, — or at any rate for not being much of a bore,—and that is, never to make a call, or talk to one person, or to several at once, for more than fifteen minutes. Fifteen minutes is not really a very long time, although it may seem so. But to apply this rule successfully one must become adept in the Fine Art of Going Away. Resting your left hand negligently on your right knee, so that the wrist protrudes with an effect of careless grace from the cuff, you have glanced at your watch and observed that the fifteen minutes are up. You get up yourself. Others get up — or, if there is but one other, she. So far, so good. But now that everybody is up, new subjects of conversation, as if catching this rising infection, come up also. You are in a position in which, except by rather too oratorical or dramatic a gesture, you cannot look at your watch; more than that, if you bore a person sitting down and wondering when you are going to get up, you bore far worse a person standing up and wondering when you will go away. That you have in effect started to go away — and not gone away — and yet must go away some time—and may go away at any minute: this consciousness, to a person standing first on one tired foot and then on the other, rapidly becomes almost, but never quite, unendurable. Reason totters, but remains on the throne. One can almost lay down a law: *Two persons who do not part with kisses should part with haste.*

## THE PERFECT GENTLEMAN

The way to do is to go like the sky-rocket — up and out.

But the fifteen-minute call followed by the flying exit is at best only a niggling and unsatisfactory solution; it is next door to always staying at home. Then certainly you would never be a bore (except to the family); but neither by any possibility could you ever be that most desirable factor in life, the Not-Bore. The Hermit is a slacker. Better far to come out of your cave, mingle, bore as little as may be — and thank Heaven that here and there you meet one whom you somehow feel reasonably certain that you do not bore.

## WHERE TOILS THE TAILOR

O F the several places in which a man waits to have something done to him, no other is so restful as the establishment of his tailor. His doctor and his dentist do their best with inviting chairs and a pile of magazines on the table: one gets an impression that both of them were once liberal subscribers to the current periodicals, but stopped a year or two ago and have never bought a magazine since. But these, in their official capacity, are painful gentlemen; and a long procession of preceding patients have imparted to the atmosphere of their waiting-rooms a heavy sense of impending misery.

The tailor is different. 'There was peace,' wrote Meredith, 'in Mr. Goren's shop. Badgered ministers, bankrupt

merchants, diplomatists with a head-
ache, — any of our modern grandees
under difficulties, — might have envied
that peace over which Mr. Goren pre-
sided: and he was an enviable man. He
loved his craft, he believed he had not
succeeded the millions of antecedent
tailors in vain.'

And so it is, I dare say, in varying
degree with all tailors; or at any rate
should be, for tailor and customer meet
on the pleasantest imaginable plane of
congenial interest. A person whose chief
desire in life at the moment is to be
becomingly dressed comes to one whose
chief ambition in life at the moment is
to becomingly dress him. No hideous
and insistent apprehension preys on
the mind of the waiting customer; for
the tailor's worst tool is a tape-measure,
and his worst discovery may be that
the customer is growing fat. One waits,

indeed, without serious apprehension, at the barber's; but here the company is mixed and the knowledge inescapable that it will look on with idle interest while he cuts your hair or covers your honest face with lather. Only the harmless necessary assistant will see you measured, and he, by long practise, has acquired an air of remoteness and indifference that makes him next thing to invisible. So complete indeed is this tactful abstraction that one might imagine him a man newly fallen in love.

I have seen it stated, though I cannot remember just where, that the Old Testament makes no mention of the tailor; the Book, however, shows plainly that Solomon was not only a sage but also a best-dresser, and it stands to reason that his wives did not make his clothes. One wife might have done it, but not three hundred. A tailor came at intervals to the palace, and then went back to where, somewhere in the business section of the ancient city, there was doubtless a tablet with a cuneiform inscription:—

> 𝕴 am he that makes the
> Glory of Solomon: yea,
> the Maker of the Upper
> and the Nether Glory.

The Smart Set of Solomon's day patronized him, yet he remained, quite naturally, beneath the notice of the Old Testament writers — unfashionable men, one may readily believe, living at a convenient period when a garment very much like our own bath-robe answered their own purposes, and could probably be bought ready-to-wear.

But one can no more think of a full-blown civilization without tailors than one can imagine a complex state of society in which, for example, the contemporary *Saturday Evening Post* would publish its Exclusive Saturday Evening Styles, and gentlemen would habitually buy their patterns by bust-measure and cut out their new suits at home on the dining-room table. The idea may seem practical, but the bust with men is evidently not a reliable guide to all the other anatomical proportions. Nor, again, however little the Old Testament concerns itself with tailors, did it fail to mention the first of them. The line goes back to Adam, cross-legged under the Tree,—the first tailor and the first customer together,—companioned, pleasantly enough, by the first 'little dressmaker.' They made their clothes together, and made them alike — an impressive, beautiful symbol of the perfect harmony between the sexes that the world lost and is now slowly regaining.

## THE PERFECT GENTLEMAN

Times have changed since Adam: the apron of his honest anxious handicraft — for it was the penalty of his sin that he would never be happy until he got it finished and put it on — has undergone many changes, in the course of which even its evolution into Plymouth Rock Pants, yes even those once seemingly eternal lines, —

> When the pant-hunter pantless
> Is panting for pants,—

are now fading from human memory; yet until within the past few decades a gentleman had a tailor as inexorably as he had a nose. But now the immemorial visit to his tailor is no longer absolutely necessary. He may, if such is his inclination, — as I am sure it would have been Adam's, — get his new suit all finished and ready-to-wear. Charley Wax, the sartorially Perfect Gentleman, smiles invitation and encouragement from many a window; an army of elegant and expeditious employees, each as much like Charley Wax as is humanly possible, waits to conduct him to a million ready-to-wear suits. His intellect is appealed to by the plausible argument that we live in a *busy time*, in which the *leaders of men* simply cannot *afford to waste* their valuable hours by going to the tailor: at the ready-to-wear emporium you simply pay your money and take your choice.

Many a gentleman, suddenly discovering that he is a 'leader of men,' has deserted his tailor: many a gentleman, learning by experience that it takes as long to try on clothes in one place as another, has presently gone back to him. Starting with the democratic premise that all men are born equal, the ready-to-wear clothier proceeds on the further assumption that each man becomes in time either short, stout, or medium; and this amendment to the Declaration of Independence has indeed created a new republic of shorts, stouts, and mediums, in which Charley Wax is the perpetual president. Here, indeed, would seem to be a step toward patterns for gentlemen: one sees the gentleman in imagination happily cutting out his new spring suit on the dining-room table, or sitting cross-legged on that centre of domestic hospitality, while he hums a little tune to himself and merrily sews the sections together.

But unfortunately the shorts, stouts, and mediums are not respectively standard according to bust-measure. A gentleman, for example, may simultaneously be short in the legs, medium in the chest, and stout in the circumference: the secret of the ready-to-wear clothier lies in his ability to meet on the spot conditions which no single pattern could hope to anticipate. We must go back toward nature, and stop short at Adam, to find a costume that any gentleman can successfully make for himself.

Personally I prefer the immemorial visit to the tailor; I like this restful atmosphere, in which unborn suits of clothes contentedly await creation in rolls of cloth, and the styles of the season are exhibited by pictures of gentlemen whose completely vacuous countenances comfortably repudiate the desirability of being 'leaders of men.' On the table the *Geographical Magazine* invites to unexciting wonder at the way other people dress. From the next room one hears the voice of the tailor, leisurely reporting to his assistant as he tape-measures a customer. In the lineage of a vocation it is odd to think that his

great-great-great grandfather might
have sat cross-legged to inspire the poem

> A carrion crow sat on an oak
> Watching a tailor shape a coat.

> 'Wife, bring me my old bent bow
> That I may shoot yon carrion crow.'

> The tailor shot, and he missed the mark,
> And shot the miller's sow through the heart.

> 'Wife, O, wife, bring brandy in a spoon,
> For the old miller's sow is in a swoon.'

The quick and unexpected tragedy (for
the sow) etches the old-time tailor at
his work: one gets, as it were, a crow's-
eye view of him. Such, I imagine, was
his universal aspect, cross-legged on a
bench in his little stall or beside his
open window, more skilled with shears
and needle than with lethal weapon,
despite the gallant brigade of tailors
who went to battle under the banner of
Queen Elizabeth. Yet I cannot imagine
my own tailor sitting cross-legged beside
an open window; nor, for that matter,

sitting cross-legged anywhere, except perhaps on the sands of the sea in his proper bathing-suit. His genealogy begins with those 'taylours' who, in the nineteenth year of Henry VII, 'sewyd the Kynge to be callyd Marchante Taylours' — evidently earning the disfavor of their neighbors, for a 'grete grudge rose among dyuers other craftys in the cyte against them.' Very soon, I fancy, these Marchante Taylours began to pride themselves on the straightness of their legs, and let subordinate craftsmen stretch their sartorious muscles. But why, as Carlyle puts it, the idea had 'gone abroad, and fixed itself down in a wide-spreading rooted error, that Tailors are a distinct species in Physiology, not Men, but fractional Parts of a Man,' nobody has yet explained satisfactorily.

So one muses, comfortably awaiting

the tailor, while the eye travels through far countries, glimpsing now and then a graceful figure that somehow reminds one of a darker complexioned September Morn, and helps perhaps to explain the wide-spread popularity of a magazine whose title seems at first thought to limit it to a public-school circulation.

And yet, strangely enough, there are men whose wives find it difficult to persuade them to go to the tailor; or, for that matter to the ready-to-wear clothier. There is, after all, something undignified in standing on a little stool and being measured; nor is it a satisfactory substitute for this procedure to put on strange garments in a little closet and come forth to pose before mirrors under the critical eye of a living Charley Wax. Fortunately the tailor and the polite and expeditious salesman of the ready-to-wear emporium have this in common:

art or nature has in both cases produced a man seemingly with no sense of humor. Fortunately, too, in both cases a gentleman goes alone to acquire a new suit. I have seen it suggested in the advertising column of the magazine that a young man should bring his fiancée with him, to help select his ready-to-wear garments; but the idea emanates from the imagination of an ad-writer, and I am sure that nobody concerned, except perhaps the fiancée, would welcome it in actual practice. Wives indeed, and maybe fiancées, sometimes accompany those they love when a hat is to be tried on and purchased; but I have been told in bitter confidence by a polite hatter that 't is a custom more honored in the breach than in the observance; and this I think is sufficient reason why it should not be extended, so to speak, to the breeches.

## SHAVING THOUGHTS

'TALKING of shaving the other night at Dr. Taylor's,' wrote the biographer Boswell, 'Dr. Johnson said, "Sir, of a thousand shavers, two do not shave so much alike as not to be distinguished." I thought this not possible, till he specified so many of the varieties in shaving, — holding the razor more or less perpendicular; drawing long or short strokes; beginning at the upper part of the face, or the under; at the right side or the left side. Indeed, when one considers what variety of sounds can be uttered by the windpipe, in the compass of a very small aperture, we may be convinced how many degrees of difference there may be in the application of the razor.'

So they talked of shaving at Dr. Taylor's before the advent of the safety-razor; and our curiosity can never be satisfied as to just what so acute an observer as Dr. Johnson would have thought of this characteristically modern invention to combine speed and convenience. I can imagine Boswell playfully reminding the doctor how that illustrious friend had quite recently expressed his disapproval of bleeding. 'Sir,' says Samuel, as he actually did on another occasion, 'courage is a quality necessary for maintaining virtue.' And he adds (blowing with high derision), 'Poh! If a man is to be intimidated by the possible contemplation of his own blood — let him grow whiskers.' At any rate among a thousand shavers to-day, two do not think so much alike that one may not be influenced by this consideration, and regard Byron, composing his verses while shaving, as a braver poet than if he had performed the operation with a safety.

The world of shavers is divided into three classes: the ordinary shaver, the safety shaver, and the extraordinary-safety shaver, who buys each safety razor as soon as it is invented and is never so happy as when about to try a new one. To a shaver of this class, cost is immaterial. A safety-razor for a cent, with twenty gold-monogramed blades and a guaranty of expert surgical attendance if he cuts himself, would stir his active interest neither more nor less than a safety-razor for a hundred dollars, with one Cannotbedull blade and an iron-clad agreement to pay the makers an indemnity if he found it unsatisfactory. He buys them secretly, lest his wife justly accuse him of extravagance, and practises cunning in getting rid of them afterward; for to a conscientious gentleman throwing away a razor is a responsible matter. It is hard to think of any place where a razor-blade, indestructible and horribly sharp as it is, — for all purposes except shaving, — can be thrown away without some worry over possible consequences. A baby may find and swallow it; the ashman sever an artery; dropping it overboard at sea is impracticable, to say nothing of the danger to some innocent fish. Mailing it anonymously to the makers, although it is expensive, is a solution, or at least shifts the responsibility. Perhaps the safest course is to put the blades with the odds and ends you have been going to throw away to-morrow ever since you can remember; for there, while you live, nobody will ever disturb them. Once, indeed, I — but this is getting too personal: I was simply about to say that it is possible to purchase a twenty-five cent safety-razor, returnable if unsatisfactory, and find the place of sale vanished before you can get back to it. But between inventions in safety-razors, the extraordinary-safety shaver is likely to revert to first principles and the naked steel of his ancestors.

And as he shaves he will perhaps think sometimes of the unhappy Edward II of England, who, before his fall, wore his beard in three corkscrew curls — and was shaved afterward by a cruel jailer who had it done *with cold water!* The fallen monarch wept with discomfort and indignation. 'Here at least,' he exclaimed reproachfully, 'is warm water on my cheeks, whether you will or no.' But the heartless shave proceeded. Razed away were those corkscrew curls from the royal chin, and so he comes down to us without

them, shaved as well as bathed in tears
— one of the most pitiful figures in
history.

Personally, however, I prefer to think
of kindlier scenes while shaving. Nothing that I can do now can help poor
Edward: no indignation of mine can
warm that cold water; perhaps, after
all, the cruel jailer had a natural and
excusable hatred of corkscrew curls anywhere. I should feel quite differently
about it if he had warmed the water;
but although a man may shave himself
with cold water, certainly nobody else
has a right to.

There have been periods in the history of man when I, too, would probably have cultivated some form of
whiskering. Perhaps, like Mr. Richard
Shute, I would have kept a gentleman
(reduced) to read aloud to me while my
valet starched and curled my whiskers

— such being the mode in the seventeenth century when Mr. Shute was what they then called, without meaning offense, a turkey merchant; and indeed his pride in his whiskers was nothing out of the common. Or, being less able to support a valet to starch and curl, and a gentleman to read aloud 'on some useful subject,' — poor gentleman! I hope that he and Mr. Shute agreed as to what subjects were useful, but I have a feeling they did n't, — I might have had to economize, and might have been one of those who were 'so curious in the management of their beards that they had pasteboard cases to put over them at night, lest they turn upon them and rumple them in their sleep.'

Nevertheless, wives continued to respect their husbands in about the normal proportion. Within the relatively brief compass of the sixteenth and seventeenth centuries, I, who would have gone smooth-shaven in the fourteenth, could conceivably have fluttered in at least thirty-eight separate and beautiful arrangements of moustaches, beard, and whiskers. Nor, I suspect, did these arrangements always wait upon the slow processes of nature. One does not *have* to grow whiskers. Napoleon's youthful officers were fiercely bewhiskered, but often with the aid of helpfully adhesive gum; and in the eighteen-thirties there occurs in the Boston *Transcript*, as a matter of course, an advertisement of 'gentlemen's whiskers ready-made or to order.' We see in imagination a quiet corner at the whisker's, with a mirror before which the Bostonian tries on his ready-made whiskers before ordering them sent home; or again, the Bostonian in doubt, selecting now this whisker, now that from the *Gentlemen's Own Whisker Book*, and still with a shade of indecision on his handsome face as he holds it up to be measured. 'Perhaps, after all, those *other* whiskers —'

But the brisk, courteous person with the dividers and tape-measure is reassuring. 'Elegant whiskers!' he repeats at intervals. 'They will do us both credit.'

The matter has, in fact, been intelligently studied; the beautifying effect of whiskers reduced to principles. If my face is too wide, a beard lengthens it; if my face is too narrow, it expands as if by magic with the addition of what have sometimes been affectionately called 'mutton chops,' or 'siders'; if my nose projects, almost like a nose trying to escape from a face to which it has been sentenced for life, a pair of large, handsome moustaches will provide a proper entourage — a nest, so to speak, on which the nose rests contentedly, almost like a setting hen; if my nose retreats backward into my face, the æsthetic solution is obviously galways. A stout gentleman can do wonders with his appearance by adopting a pointed beard, and a suit of clothes, shirt, necktie, and stockings with pronounced vertical stripes. A thin one, on the other hand, becomes at once substantial in effect, without being gross, if he cultivates side-whiskers, and wears a suit of clothes, shirt, cravat, and stockings with pronounced horizontal stripes. If my face lacks fierceness and dynamic force, it needs a brisk, arrogant moustache; or if it has too much of these qualities, a long, sad, drooping moustache will counterbalance them. I read in my volume of *Romantic Love and Personal Beauty* that 'the movements of the moustache are dependent on the muscle called *depressor alæ nasi*. By specially cultivating this muscle, men might in course of time make the movements of the moustache subject to voluntary control.'

Just think what a capacity for emotional expression lies in such a simple organ as the dog's caudal appendage, aptly called the 'psychographic tail' by Vischer; and moustaches are double, and therefore equal to two psychographic appendages! Truly I know not of which to think first — a happy gentleman wagging his moustache or a happy dog wagging two tails. And yet here am I, shaving away the daily effort of this double psychographic appendage to become visible! One might almost think that my *depressor alæ nasi* was a vermiform appendix.

It has been said by some critics that

whiskers are a disguise. I should be unwilling to commit myself to this belief;
nor can I accept the contrary conviction
that whiskers are a gift of Almighty
Providence in which the Giver is so sen-
sitively interested that to shave them
off is to invite eternal punishment of
a kind — and this, I think, destroys the
theory — that would singe them off in
about two seconds. Whiskers are real,
and sometimes uncomfortably earnest;
the belief that they betoken an almost
brutal masculine force is visible in this,
that those whose whiskers are naturally
thinnest take the greatest satisfaction
in possessing them — seem, in fact, to
say proudly, '*These* are my whiskers!'
But I cannot feel that a gentleman is
any more disguised by his whiskers,
real, ready-made, or made to order,
than he would be if he appeared naked
or in a ready-made or made-to-order

suit. Whiskers, in fact, are a subtle revelation of real character, whether the kind that exist as a soft, mysterious haze about the lower features or such as inspired the immortal limerick, — I quote from memory, —

> There was an old man with a beard
> Who said, 'I am greatly afeard
>      Two larks and a hen,
>      A jay and a wren,
> Have each made a nest in my beard.

Yet I feel also, and strongly, that the man who shaves clean stands, as it were, on his own face.

We have, indeed, but to visualize clearly the spectacle of a gentleman shaving himself and put beside it the spectacle of a gentleman starching and curling his whiskers, to see the finer personal dignity that has come with the general adoption of the razor. I am not going to attempt to describe a gentle-

man starching and curling his whiskers,
— it would be too horrible, — but I like
to dwell on the shaver. He whistles or
perhaps hums. He draws hot water
from the faucet — Alas, poor Edward!
He makes a rich, creamy lather either
in a mug or (for the sake of literary
directness) on his own with a shaving-
stick. He strops his razor, or perhaps
selects a blade already sharpened for
his convenience. He rubs in the lather.
He shaves, and, as Dr. Johnson so
shrewdly pointed out that night at Dr.
Taylor's, 'Sir, of a thousand shavers,
two do not shave so much alike as not
to be distinguished.' Perhaps he cuts
himself, for a clever man at self-muti-
lation can do it, even with a safety;
but who cares? Come, Little Alum, the
shaver's friend, smartly to the rescue!
And then, he exercises the shaver's
prerogative and powders his face.

Fortunately the process does not always go so smoothly. There are times when the Local Brotherhood of Razors have gone on strike and refuse to be stropped. There are times at which the twelve interchangeable blades are hardly better for shaving than twelve interchangeable postage-stamps. There are times when the lather might have been fairly guaranteed to dry on the face. There are times when Little Alum, the shaver's friend, might well feel the sting of his own powerlessness. But these times are the blessed cause of genial satisfaction when everything goes happily.

Truly it is worth while to grow a beard — for the sake of shaving it off. Not such a beard as one might starch and curl — but the beginnings — an obfuscation of the chin, cheeks, and upper lip — a horror of unseemly growth — a

## SHAVING THOUGHTS

landscape of the face comparable to

> that ominous tract which, all agree,
> Hides the Dark Tower

in Browning's grim poem of 'Childe Roland.' *Then* is the time to strop your favorite razor! I wonder, while stropping mine, if any man still lives who uses a moustache cup?

## OH, THE AFTERNOON TEA!

ANY man who knows that, sooner or later, he must go to another afternoon tea cannot but rejoice at the recent invention of an oval, platter-like saucer, large enough to hold with ease a cup, a lettuce or other sandwich, and a dainty trifle of pastry. The thing was needed: the modesty of the anonymous inventor — evidently *not* Mr. Edison — reveals him one of the large body of occasional and unwilling tea-goers. We, the reluctant and unwilling, are all strangely alike at these functions; and we have all been embarrassed by the old-fashioned saucer. Circular in shape, and hardly larger than the cup that belies its reputation and dances drunkenly whenever another guest joggles our elbow, — which happens so often that we suspect conspiracy, — the old-fashioned saucer affords no reasonably secure perch for a sandwich; responds with delight to the law of gravitation if left to itself; and sets us wishing, those of us who think scientifically, that evolution had refrained from doing away with an extension by which alone we could now hope to manage it. *We mean a tail!* If afternoon teas had been started in the Oligocene Epoch instead of the seventeenth century, we are convinced that evolution, far from discarding this useful appendage, would have perfected it. A little hand would have evolved at the end of it — such a one as might hold a Perfect Gentleman's saucer while he sipped from his tea-cup.

Nay, more. In many ways that will at once occur to the intelligent reader this little hand would be helpful in our complex modern civilization. It would hold this essay. It would turn the music at the piano. It would enable two well-disposed persons cordially to shake hands when their four other hands were busy with bundles. It would slap the coward mosquito that stabs in the back. It would be absolutely perfect for waving farewell. Nor would there be anything 'funny' about it, or shocking to the most refined sensibilities: the vulgar would laugh and the refined would hide a shudder at the sight of a man with no tail! We would, of course, all look like the Devil, but everybody knows that *his* tail has never yet kept him out of polite society.

This digression, however, leads us away from our subject into alien regrets. We put it behind us.

The truth is, we do not like your afternoon teas — except those little ones, like the nice children of an objectionable mother, that are informal, intimate, and not destructive of our identity. At larger gatherings we have no identity: we are supernumeraries, mere tea-cup bearers, wooden Indians who have been through Hampton, hand-carved gentlemen, automaton tea-goers. In short, we are so many lay figures, each with a tea-cup in one hand and food in the other; we know that we are smiling because we can feel it; we remain where we are laid until forcibly moved to another spot, and we are capable, under pressure, of emitting a few set phrases that resemble human speech.

Yet within this odd simulacrum of a worldly, entertaining, and interested gentleman, a living mind surveys the gay scene with a strange, emotionless detachment — just so, perhaps, will it eventually survive the body. We are really alive, conscious that we dislike change, nervous when moved and stood up in another place, and intellectually certain that no real harm can come to us. One is reminded of Seneca's observation: *Vere magnum, habere fragilitatem hominis, securitatem dei.* There is about us something of the frailty of a man, something of the security of a god; the pity of it is that we cannot follow Seneca to his conclusion and comfort ourselves with the thought that we are 'truly great.'

I have often wondered, while 'dolling up,' as the strikingly appropriate modernism puts it, for such a function, whether there is any universal reason why a reluctant man should go to an afternoon tea. There are, of course, many individual reasons, more or less important to the individual tea-goer; but for us the impulsion comes inevitably from without. The verb 'drag,' often applied to the process by which a man is brought to a tea, indicates how valuable would be the discovery of a Universal Reason wherefore any man might hope to derive some personal good from this inescapable experience.

An excellent place for the thinker to examine this problem is in his bath-tub preparatory to dolling up. He is alone and safe from interruption, unless he has forgotten to lock the door; his memory and observation of afternoon teas past is stimulated by afternoon tea to come; and he is himself more like the Universal Man than on most other occasions. Featherless biped mammals that we are, what need have we in common that might conceivably provide a good and sufficient reason for the dolling up to which I am about to subject myself? Substantial food, less fleeting, however, than a lettuce or other sandwich and a dainty trifle of pastry; protective clothing; a house, or even a cave, to shelter us in cold or stormy weather — these, evidently, are clearly apprehended necessities, and we will march on the soles of our feet, like the plantigrade creatures we are, wherever such goods are obtainable.

If all men were hungry, naked, and homeless, and the afternoon tea provided food, clothes, and a home, any man would jump at an invitation. But there are other necessities of living — and here, too, I in my porcelain dish am one with Christopher Columbus, Lord Chesterfield, Chang the Chinese Giant, the Editor of the *Atlantic*, and the humblest illiterate who never heard of him — of which we are not so vividly conscious. Yet we seek them instinctively, each in his own manner and degree — amusement, useful experience, friends, and his own soul. So I read and accept Tagore when he says, 'Man's history is the history of man's journey to the unknown in quest of his immortal self — his soul.' Willy-nilly, even higglety-pigglety and helter-skelter, these are what the featherless biped is after.

As for useful experience, this afternoon tea reminds me of those lower social gatherings where liquor is, or used to be, sold only to be drunk on the premises. Granting that I become a finished tea-goer, easy of speech, nodding, laughing, secure in the graceful manipulation of my tea-things, never upsetting my tea, never putting my sandwich in the way of an articulating tongue, yet is all this experience of no use whatever to me except at other afternoon teas. I go to school simply to learn how to go to school. The most finished and complete tea-goer, if he behaves anywhere else as he does at an afternoon tea, creates more widely the same unfavorable impression that he creates, in his own proper sphere, on me. Can I then reasonably regard experience as useful which I observe to be useful only for doing something which I observe to be useless? The soap agrees that I cannot. Yet, says the sponge, *if* I might hope at some afternoon tea to discover my immortal soul, the case would be different; this experience would be valuable. O foolish sponge! I am compelled to tell you that at afternoon teas it is especially difficult for a mortal gentleman to believe that he has any immortal soul to look for. It is a gathering essentially mundane and ephemeral. For it we put on our most worldly garments. For it we practise our most worldly smirks in dumb rehearsal before our mirror and

an audience of one silly, attentive im-
age, thinking that this time, this time
— But it is always the same: the ob-
servant mind in the immovable body.
As for the immortal soul, O sponge! it
may, and doubtless does, go to strange
places — but it *cannot be dragged.*

And so we come to the final question:
is the afternoon tea a place where one
featherless, plantigrade, biped mammal
of the genus *Homo* may meet another
whom he might hope some time to call
a friend? I do not mean 'my friend
What's-his-name?' but rather such another biped as Tennyson had in mind
when he wrote, —

> Since we deserved the name of friends
> And thine effect so lives in me,
> A part of mine may live in thee
> And move thee on to noble ends.

I grant you, peering out of my tub at
the world, that there are many to whom

this thought sounds sublimated and extravagant: a poet says this sort of thing because such is his poetic business. We come nearer perhaps to the universal understanding in John Hay's definition that 'Friends are the sunshine of life'; for it is equally true that all men seek sunlight and that every man seeks a friend after his own kind and nature. The best and most intelligent of us admit the rarity and value of friendship; the worst and most ignorant of us are unwittingly the better for knowing some friendly companion. But these afternoon teas are inimical to friendship; and the first duty of a hostess is to separate, expeditiously and without hope of again coming together, any other two guests who appear to be getting acquainted. On this count, even were we not Automaton Tea-Goers, debarred by inherent stability from any normal human intercourse, the afternoon tea must prove more disheartening than helpful. We might at best glimpse a potential friend as the desert islander sights a passing sail on the far horizon.

There is, alas, no Universal Reason why a man should go to an afternoon tea!

So the matter looks to me in my tub, but perhaps, like Diogenes, I am a cynic philosopher. After all, when a thing cannot be escaped, why seek for reasons not to escape it? Let us, rather, be brave if we cannot be gay; cheerful if we cannot talk; ornamental if we cannot move. As the grave-digger in Elsinore churchyard might say: 'Here lies the afternoon tea; good: here stands the gentleman; good: If the gentleman go to this afternoon tea and bore himself, it is, will he, nill he, he goes, — mark you that? But if the afternoon tea come to him and bore him, he bores not himself; argal, he that goes not willingly to the afternoon tea wearies not his own life.'

So, in effect, he that is *dragged* to an afternoon tea does not go at all; and when he gets there, he is really somewhere else. This happy thought is a little difficult to reconcile with circumstances; but when one has become thoroughly soaked in it, it is a great help.

THE END